POETRY PLAIN AND SIMPLE

Ingeborg Zauels Seymour

Prospect Press
Sistersville, WV
New York, NY

Published by Prospect Press
609 Main Street
Sistersville, West Virginia 26175

Library of Congress Catalog Card Number:
99-070497

ISBN: 1-892668-10-6

Manufactured in the United States of America

First Edition

10 9 8 7 6 5 4 3 2 1

I dedicate this book of poetry to my mother,
sister Marianne, brother Josef and
friends Lana & John.

INTRODUCTION AND CREDITS

My poem "A Country Parade" was certified as semi-finalist in the 1996 North American Open Poetry Contest by The National Library of Poetry. On November 1, 1996 I was elected into "The International Poetry Hall of Fame." The Ingeborg Seymour Poetry exhibit is on permanent display as part of The International Poetry Hall of Fame's Museum on the Internet's World Wide Web. Also, I received the Editor's Choice Award for Outstanding Achievement in Poetry from The National Library of Poetry for 1997 and again in 1998.

ANTHOLOGIES

The Colors of Thought
By The National Library of Poetry, 1996

Best Poems of 1998
By The National Library of Poetry

Outstanding Poets of 1998
By The National Library of Poetry

Poetic Voices of America, Spring 1998
By Sparrowgrass Poetry Forum

Ten Years of Excellence 1988-1998
By Sparrowgrass Poetry Forum

CONTENTS

PRECIOUS GIFT OF FRIENDSHIP

How wonderful life could be,
if there was friendship and love for you and me.
Kind words, trust in one another and honesty,
all the above would be just fine with me.

To watch the sunrise in the morning,
and the sunset in the evening.
Saying hi to Mr. Moon at night,
and loving the beauty of all the stars.
Looking at the heavens with fond thoughts and memories
of loved ones and friends who reside there.

Time is so precious, and life so short.
Let's not waste a moment,
for we cannot recall one minute at all.
So from this moment forward,
let there be love, faith in each other,
hope and peace as we have known before
and will not fuss any more.
Let's count our blessings!

If memories could speak,
how I would love to listen what they had to say.
About the valleys and mountains,
we had to conquer along our way.
There were good times, and not so good times.
But you see dear friend, you were my anchor.
No matter how big the problem, you gave me a helping hand.
Without questions asked, your big heart gave me
a shoulder to cry on.
You see dear friend, your wisdom and understanding
made big problems almost disappear.
How could I ever thank you, just know I do
appreciate you for all you have done.
You are my Guardian Angel, I thank the Lord
for sending you into my life.
You see God loves you, and so do I.
There may be detours in everyone's life,
and when these detours come our way
all we can say is why?
But there is a reason for everything in life,
perhaps it is a lesson to realize
that nothing lasts forever.
Except all the wonderful memories,
that *NO ONE* can take away!

SPRING AT LAST

One beautiful sunny morning,
shy little Lily of the valley started to ring.
Wake up all my friends the flowers,
we have lots of work to do for hours.
Let's make the gardens look pretty.
Said the tulip, gee you are witty.
Hurry said the trees, let's show our leaves.
The roses became busy.
The bushes worked hard not to look lazy.
The powerful friend of all life on earth said:
I will give you lots of sunshine,
for I am proud of you, you are all mine.
Said the clouds, hey, don't forget about us,
as you know, without rain where would you be?
Then Mr. Wind blew a message, how strong it was,
for, without him, it all would be a lost cause.
Let's not forget the moon and the stars at night,
for they take over so each of you can rest.
Now that all have joined together,
let's wish and hope for perfect weather.
And that the people we worked so hard for,
will give us tender care and love to the core.
Oh, listen to the birds singing and chirping in the trees,
it surely sounds like a true masterpiece!

Springtime, summer, fall or winter,
the place to go in this country is the Southeast.
Believe me, to be there would be quite a feast.
The island I speak of is shaped like a shoe,
and being there will be an eye filling for you.
Perhaps you have heard of the island called Hilton Head,
surely some of you have been there I bet.
Along the shore of South Carolina,
where the water is fine, where the beaches invite ya.
To relax and dream and see for miles,
all this beauty will be a treat for your eyes.
Once you are there, you feel you found a treasure,
that is of nature, which no one can measure.
Just watch the sunset reflect on the ocean,
looks like pure gold, what a sight, there is nothing in motion.
The shore birds so playful in water and the sand,
people so friendly, you could think you found a friend.
If golf is your game, play there, you might have a chance
at fame. Should tennis be your pleasure,
participate at your leisure.
Even bicycle rides are in order,
while driving along enjoy listening to your radio or recorder
walking along the shore is relaxing and so much more.
Such as sailboats on the water while trying to
harness the wind.
Nothing can compare with all you see,
especially southern hospitality.
The island saturated with flowers and trees,
many oak trees with hanging moss on their vine.
If you are lucky, perhaps you see an alligator
enjoy sunshine.
Yes, I trust that I described all I was in awe about.
This paradise my friends call home,
Is "The Jewel of the South".

Amid the Nevada Desert, there is a treasure to be seen!
The best things in life are free,
there to admire and enjoy by you and me.
Let's realize and not take for granted,
and find in Mother Nature what we always wanted.
A short drive from Las Vegas, away from the lights.
Take a ride toward Red Rock Mountain,
once you were there you will return again.
The early morning sun with blue sky and pretty clouds
will set the stage for you,
beauty that seldom is found, and that is true.
Suddenly there appears the view of a natural masterpiece!
When first I saw it, tears came into my eyes,
I just can not describe this surprise.
How humble I became and instantly I knew,
such perfection and such a sight My Lord only could do.
Mother Nature carefully created this glamour,
without using a chisel and hammer.
Layers across the mountains in colors so vivid,
a perfect artist with his or her brush can not capture it.
At the Vista Point three metal plaques describe the history,
of hundreds of years ago, they tell quite a story.
In the desert at times some donkeys will greet you,
which were left behind, after the Miners were through.
To be and spend some time at this beautiful place
will bring a happy expression to everyone's face!

A RAINY MORNING

Rain oh rain I welcome you, the sound is oh so fine,
since mostly you visit where I live, is at wintertime.
All vegetation will breathe a deep sigh,
through the summer water was in short supply.
The request was to conserve the liquid as good as gold,
Many lawns looked so bad while the heat did unfold.
Precious raindrops all life depends on you,
without you, what would the entire world do?
We can not tell you how and when to give us water,
the elements decide for you that mighty power.
All animals that depend on green pasture feed,
must feel good, the water will help to reseed.
A thank you to the clouds, for they are your transportation,
wherever you drift, through the world including our nation.
You try to bring us clean and healthy water,
but all industries have different ideas on order.
Some people feel sad when rain comes to this earth,
there can not only be sunshine, as we know what you are
worth.
So please, visit us whenever you can manage,
that is in moderation, for too much of you does great damage.
The Lord knew when he created the elements,
for they control this planet at their own segments.

FIRST SNOW OF THE YEAR

While sleeping Mother Nature worked hard on a surprise,
when I awoke, looking out my window there was a treat for
my eyes.
The snow had fallen what a sudden change took place,
the mountains around me and as far I could see had a
different face.
It looks so peaceful, quiet and serene,
the snow covered everything that yesterday was green.
Every roof top so pretty with smoke leaving the chimney,
inside the fireplace displaying flames dancing as done to a
melody.
Admiring the carpet of virgin white snow,
makes me feel that is where I would like to go .
Seeing my dogs walking through "The White God-Send",
leaving original markings which will disappear, their paw
prints.
Here and there are signs that birds had been here as well,
most likely they were looking for food I could tell.
Nature can be hard at wintertime,
for people and any kind of life,
causing difficulty and making it hard to survive.
For children snow is something beautiful to play in,
that is the innocence of being young, adults are saying.
As I write the snow starts falling again,
just like our fingerprints, no two snow flakes are the same.
Each tree and bush has a pretty white design,
like a painting, it will leave a memory so divine.

Yes, Love can be a complicated state of mind.
Thinking only with our heart, will not always work we will find.
From a child love is pure, without conditions.
For many teenagers love is not thinking with long-term visions.
When it comes to adults, it often combines all of the above.
But when we become seniors, what is life without kindness and love?
What happened to loyalty, I guess it lost its meaning.
Friends are important in all of our lives.
Unconditional love from pets, maybe a dog or cat.
As a popular president said "If you want a friend for life get a dog."
Just saying "I love you" and not meaning it with your heart,
could cause problems that perhaps we could regret.
There is love for music, which soothes the mind.
Do not forget Mother Nature which is beautiful and kind.
Most important is love for life and happiness.
We have forgotten the significance of caring, giving and forgiving,
which are so important for our daily living.
Then there is commitment, that means in sickness and health,
along life's way through struggle and acquiring wealth.
So let's cherish the good and happy times,
and enjoy life to the fullest, whatever rings our chimes.
Over the years my dear mother impressed unto me,
live life by the Golden Rule!
Meaning what you do not wish to be done to you,
do not do unto others!
Then we can say we tried our best,
until the end of our lives, when we are laid to our final rest.

Oh Lord, thank you for giving me sight, so I can admire
all that is perfect, done by your might.
When you created this earth, you had the perfect master plan,
where and what you needed, no one else can.
By the hands of the greatest sculpture, who controlled how
this world should be. The wisdom of our master knew
how all things would work in harmony.
You chose just where to put the oceans, then placed the rivers
and lake. You had this notion for without water nothing living
could exist. There again you were the specialist.
With your knowledge you decided there should be mountains.
Then you made room for the deserts, which are important in
this world.
So there would be food for us, we ungrateful humans,
you filled the waters with fish and plant life.
The mountains with trees, bushes and greens,
so all the animals and fowl had shelter.
Of course by hunting we humans could have food and
clothing.
The deserts served their purpose, as you know so well.
With everything you did for us Lord, we simple took for
granted.
You knew exactly what we would need,
but the people of this planet discovered greed.
We exploited all the treasures,
you dear father supplied by great measures.
If this goes on without your supervision,
well, then look out population of this earth,
there will come an uncontrollable big collision.
As we know "As the End" for all life of this world.

From childhood through the rest of our lives,
we were told it is important to trust and not to listen to lies.
A child with his or her smile will capture,
the kindness of an ice cold heart, and make it to rapture.
Trust means to like, love or feeling close to a human being,
when this happens, we feel like singing!
Trusting someone makes you feel good and happy.
Some people we believe are lovers or friend,
they abuse our trust, and their interest is only that they feel content.
You see, many of us forget the need to trust someone in our lives,
when life is comfortable, we forget and close our eyes.
We tend to cut out our memories, which we cherished through the years,
for selfish reasons people plan their own affairs.
To love and trust blindly is a mistake,
you get excuses which are hard to take.
You will ask yourself why, and do not understand,
there will be a sign once you are on the mend.
Only time will heal the hurt that was done,
the saying goes, "There is someone for Everyone".
This trusting seemed so real, and would last forever, but people are clever.
Seems like the ones we love and trust most,
they will hurt us, they do act like a ghost.
So be careful when it comes to humans, they promise to be loyal,
faithful and love you until the end,
but these words are empty, like the sand running through your hand.
Only dreamers believe in unconditional love and trust,
But they will wake up to "Shattered Love and Trust".

PEOPLE

Why are people so hard to understand?
when you think you know them, then you reach a dead end.
Have we forgotten our humble beginning?
Let's take a moment and try to comprehend,
how it happened, that people of this world are winning.
There are seven continents of the earth's land,
where God placed us according to the master's hand.
He had to consider the elements so we heard.
That is why people are existing in different races,
so we survive the cold and the heat of various places.
The blue eyed light complexioned humans origin started in the North.
So brown eyed darker skinned people could take hot temperature,
God settled them in the hot parts of the continent's nature.
Our Lord knew exactly why he decided,
but we the people preferred to be divided.
As long as there are inhabitants on this earth,
some will get long, and others will make it worse.
At the beginning we received love and compassion in our heart,
later we found hate, jealousy, fear and even to hurt others would play a part.
We have difficulty to recall how to be sisters and brothers,
to think of oneself is more important than to think of others.
Material things come before they think of the family,
until that changes there can not be harmony.
Our master with love in his heart for us created,
but we just took and abused, and sometimes with hatred.
Some of us are leaders, others do follow,
so search your heart, and think of not to be so shallow.
Only then, there will be peace on earth, we will appreciate what life is worth.

This turned out to be a perfect day,
to have a parade with so many surprises all the way.
There were lots of mounted horses, even miniature mules,
seven llamas that walked proudly exactly to their cues.
Many vintage cars, fire truck and Smokey the Bear,
it was so exciting to see, and many people were there.
The streets lined with visitors young and old,
there were candies thrown from vehicles, a sight to behold.
To take care of feeling hungry, there was a hot-dog stand.
Two boys driving along the street calling "Sodas for fifty cents".
To have the perfect atmosphere there was a mariachi band,
the sound of these songs was oh so grand.
Homemade floats gave the parade that special touch,
with such nice people on them, for all of us to watch.
This is a small hamlet where the parade took place,
where neighbors and strangers still say "Hi", with a happy face.
The parade was just long enough, the time it lasted.
All was under control and went well,
so we will look forward to next year I can tell.

We have a choice in life which road to travel,
some like excitement, others look forward to security,
whichever we choose, we have to face and there will be
responsibility.
We are individuals and each life takes a different course,
all of us think that we are the captain of our own boat of
course.
Life is not perfect, but it can be good!
Sometimes it feels like a roller coaster ride,
working hard and plan for the future makes us feel full of
pride.
Then we should count our blessings of family and friends,
good people we meet along life's journey, ought to be today's
trends.
To appreciate our pets, and the wisdom that came from
experience,
the good and the bad formed our character at our own
expense.
Respect and self-respect are so important through our life,
consider the feelings of others and you will survive.
Be careful with having big ideas, and do not over extend,
the months pass by fast, and coming bills make you feel to
repent.
To younger folks I say work hard and put your thoughts into
action,
It will pay off later, there will be no worries, you will enjoy
satisfaction.
Take this example and apply to your own life,
remember, nothing is free in life, it takes an effort and done
with pride.
It takes love and understanding and consideration,
so set your compass and follow the correct direction.

You will be happy that you gave it a try,
is better to have courage than ask yourself later "Why"?
We all have failed and later succeed,
never give up and your hopes and dreams will be complete.

HONORING MY GRANDMOTHER!

As a child I could tell that her love was real,
for Grandma was never wrong did I feel.
No matter what happened, she would understand,
and still today I say, when she died, I lost my best friend.
When she was so ill toward the end,
I remember she asked me to plant forget-me-nots on her grave,
you see she always faced things and never did pretend.
I promised Grandma that I would,
and with my mother's help I really could.

I was ten years old when I lost her,
I cried and I missed her, and wished she was still there.
But God needed her, she was a good person,
she was generous, her kind heart would give a helping hand
without reason.

A few weeks after Grandma's passing,
my mother reminded me of the promise I made.
So mother and daughter to the nursery they went,
to buy the most beautiful forget-me-nots,
you see, for my Grandma they were meant.

To the grave we went, and with my little hands I planted,
the forget-me-nots my Oma had wanted.
My memories are so vivid after all these years,
and thinking of Grandma made me shed some tears.

To the children of today I say,
Love your Grandmas.
Even if they seem old fashioned in their way.
Grandma in her heart has love for you,
which is sincere and true!
So give respect and love in return,
Grandma's life could be short.
It would be easier when the day comes that you will mourn.

And to my Oma, that means Grandma in German,
I say thank you!
I loved you so much as a child could then,
and from my heart I say "Auf Wiedersehen."

A BARREN PIECE OF LAND

The piece of land is one acre,
though full of weeds then, was created by our maker.
When purchased, the thought was to perhaps build a house,
there were rabbits, squirrels and sometimes a mouse.
Years later finally I put my thoughts into action,
what all would be involved to have total satisfaction.
To hire a contractor and permits had to be gotten,
the planning took time, so nothing was forgotten.
How exciting the time was when the house was being built,
lots of photos were taken, of every section to be filled.
Now that the home I dreamed of was involved,
the weeds around it had to be resolved.
But with our pioneer spirit we acquired many trees,
My mother and I planted them, also bulbs and various seeds.
After all had taken place, which took hard working hours,
when spring arrived, what a joy to see all these flowers.
The roses so colorful in deep red and hot pink,
we forgot about the hard work then, I think!
There are various bushes, grapes and a peach tree,
when the first fruits ripened, we were in awe you see.
Now nine years later since it all began,
today the trees are tall, they grew so since then.
It started with a challenge and a dream years ago,
but determination and faith helped make it so.
I am filled with pride when I admire all this beauty,
it was not easy always, but I did my duty.

I was a child when World War II began,
I grew to be a teenager when the war came to an end.
Then Germany was occupied by four different nations,
The Rhineland where my family resided,
was occupied by the British and Americans so was decided.
In time I learned about America, the land of opportunity,
from Americans that were in love with their country you see.
I was anxious to hear what they had to say,
it sounded so great, in thoughts, I was already on my way.
In poor English I wrote a letter with a photo enclosed,
to "Y-W-C-A" in New York, asking total strangers if they could help me find a sponsor.
What a surprise, three weeks later a letter from Mrs. Staelin came,
telling me that she would help me, and this was not a game.
I had to send references, which she accepted.
So my dream was starting to begin, there were quotas, it took three years
until I departed for the U.S.A., but I shed quite a few tears.
Looking back I realize that it took a lot of courage,
but it was worth it, life always has a message.
I was so lucky that God sent so many good people into my life.
Seeing the New York skyline and Statue of Liberty,
pointed out to me by a stranger then, and today is my best friend.
Many things have changed in 47 years I am here,
but if one works hard, there are opportunities to share.
There may be despair, but never give up, for I say to you,
keep on dreaming for "Dreams Do Come True".

HI THERE!

Hi there, permit me to say "Hello" to you,
you look familiar, is it possible that you remember me too?
For years I wondered where you could be,
did your thoughts ever let you think of me?
When we cared for each other, we were so young.
Had we known then what life's journey would teach us,
would we make the same mistake or would we reach for the
stars?
How great it is to see you again,
could we talk for a while now and then?
You said yes?
How happy that makes me feel,
I mean it with all my heart, and that is for real.
Thank you God for this re-union.
Teach my heart to be happy for always,
through happy times and troublesome days.
This sounds like a dream come true,
if it is, I wish the same for you.
Now time will tell if we can feel as way back then,
but the years have changed us, should we try again?
The tooth of time is showing in our faces,
we both once were happy but we moved to different places.
Each of us has to take life one day at a time,
tomorrow may not come, so goes the rhyme.
So cherish all memories, the good and happy times,
they will comfort us through rain and when the sun shines.

Good morning Lord, what a beautiful day,
thank you for the sunshine you send my way.
What a lovely sound coming from a tree,
little bird I love the song you whistle for me.
Sorry I can not call you by name, you make me feel happy just the same.
Stay and visit for a while, your happy songs do make me smile.
Here come papa and mama quail with their brood,
How protective the instructions the babies do give a hoot.
Such love shown by the quails' parents!
Humans could truly take notice and pay attention,
but why should they, we do not like intervention.
Many people do not seem to care, all they want is what to do and where.
If only we the people would daily stop and think,
perhaps meditation would prevent seeing a shrink.

WAKE UP CALL

All of this crime simply has to come to an end,
daily happenings so terrible I cannot comprehend.
To all of us this should be a wake up call,
there still is time to reverse it all.
Starting with parents to watch and listen to their children,
to take notice of their behavior and a little time,
it might even help and prevent a crime.
Set a good example and do not use drugs,
they give you unreal promises, and cost you a lot of bucks.
Children are gullible, and always look for a friend.
Remember, drugs are no candies,
guns are no toys and alcohol is no pacifier,
you may think it will satisfy your desire.
Joining a gang is dangerous,
living carelessly makes no sense.
God meant only good for us, and no nonsense.
Children and young adults belong in school,
the streets do not give you a home, they make a fool of you.
Let's become family oriented again,
the excuse of finding myself, is just playing a game.
Let's enjoy life what it is all about,
our nation would be healthy, let's give a big shout.
After all this is what this country is all about!

Looking back over the years and happy hours,
that all our pets brought to us because they were ours.
My first dog's name was Baby, she was the runt of the litter,
she was left behind and looked so alone, nobody would take
her.
Looking at me with those beautiful big brown eyes,
instantly I knew she was mine, what a surprise.
She lived a full life with us and I shall never forget her!
Then into our home came Liebchen, Michelle and Susie,
three poodles a teacup, toy, and miniature,
each had a different personality, with so much love for family
and me.
It was so hard to lose them, you see they were close in age,
they were our companions and family members, all that was
left was an empty travel cage.
Not wanting to be alone I adopted Candy and Baby II
destined to die,
I am so glad I took them, they fill my home with love, I have
no reason to cry.
To see my two dogs playing with Bessy "The Kitty Cat",
just warms my heart, why can't people get along like that?
My Candy, Baby II and I belong in the category of being
seniors,
our hair has become silver, we like it, we had good years.
Bessy the kitty, is full of pep and loves to play,
so the doggies and I will do our best to comply.
There also was handsome "Fluffy" my mother's best friend
how she loved him, both took that final journey, both are
content.
The love and loyalty of a pet is unconditional,
all they long for is good care and a kind word that comes
natural.
If pets were neutered or spayed, it would be a kind deed,
thousands would be spared the agony and euthanasia no
need.

CONSIDER PEOPLE'S FEELINGS!

Each and everyone of us has feelings I will describe!

Often times people's feelings are abused by unkind words,
let's stop and think before someone hurts.

The wonderful feeling of being in love,
is like a blessing from the Lord above.
We feel happy when things go right,
feeling sad sometimes we have to fight.
At times our way comes a surprise,
feeling jealous often shows in our eyes.
We also experience that we feel lonely,
remembering good and happy times will erase that only.

Showing love and compassion can make one feel humble.
Greed and being selfish changes a person's character,
being generous and caring fills one with laughter.
The feeling of being grateful and also proud,
restores contentment, your heart will beat loud.

After feeling cold, heat is so welcome.
Food will take away the pain of being hungry,
after a while feeling full we become sleepy.
There are times that we are angry,
but never out of control, or it could lead into lots of worry,
so let us show kindness and respect to each other.

Yes, the word Faith covers every part of our life,
when truly practiced, Faith will help us to survive.
We take the good life and our health for granted,
but unexpected happenings appear when they are not wanted.
We humans think nothing bad will ever happen,
we are the driver in our life, but God is our captain.
Sometimes everyone's life will be tested,
to see where our strength lies and is manifested.
The daily life can bring disappointments,
too hard to take we can not express with simple comments.
We will struggle for a while but sometimes can not fix.
The Faith we have in mankind and people we love,
when it seems overwhelming I pray to the Lord above.
He heard me when I was scared and feeling low,
something lifted my spirit and I gladly tell you so.

The five letters that spell FAITH:

F — Tells us not to fear.
A — Amen we say at the end when we pray.
I — Means believing in myself all the way.
T — Troubles will subside if we give it a chance.
H — Will deliver hope to us, perhaps even dance.

The one who gives Faith to us is God!

G — Means good.
O — Starts the word overcome.
D — Beginning the word "Dear", meaning love,
and that is what God sends to all of us.

As long as our planet does exist,
there were wars to confront while they did persist.
The Bible tells the story of brothers Abel and Cain,
even then siblings displayed power hard to explain.
Parents dream that their children's knowledge be shown,
since this world was created, how many monsters have we known?
Yes, there can be a flaw in human nature,
no one is perfect on earth, the only one is our creator.
Just look at our children, their beauty and untapped resources,
we live in the Jet-Age it takes years to develop their minds' courses.
This is the superficial generation where many families fall apart,
if not stopped by parents their children by example take to heart.
Why not take time to smell the roses and enjoy the beauty of nature,
one becomes filled with peace, love and realize to be more mature.
God gave us a brain so let's use it, try less use of TV,
when tried and experienced, you will feel different you see.
The whole world would be a happier place,
if the leaders remembered what mother asked for when saying grace.
Women are mostly gentle, and men often are powerful and strong,
why not be natural, women do cry and men are told it is wrong.
It would be great for all we humans to share the good within us,
people would be real again, and the world be rid of all the fuss.
Do research into healing desperately ill and confused people,
and not for destruction of the human race, for it would be evil.
Combine all the knowledge of the world's information,
too much money changes a person's mind, let's explore education !

As a child I loved to watch Butterflies,
they were so colorful and their movements caught my eyes.
I tried to catch them, but at no avail,
they were faster and knew how to choose their own trail.
When I see Butterflies today, they bring memories of my
childhood!
Children do not understand how all this beauty began,
as an adult I say "Thank you Lord", when Butterflies come
now and then.
Just to think as a tiny larva your life evolved,
in a short time you grew and became pretty, and the miracle
was resolved.
Now you are ready and fully grown,
take care of yourself, for you are on your own!
You will leave us people for your own destination,
I wish you farewell and without hesitation.
I shall remember all your beauty while visiting my flowers,
truly, when it is about nature, I could watch for hours.

BEAUTIFUL RAINBOW

After the rain the air smells so clean,
at times there is a beautiful rainbow to be seen.
No two rainbows are the same in color or shape.
While watering my flowers partial rainbows appear
looking so gorgeous like a friend dropped by to share.
I was told to make a wish when a rainbow I see,
there were many wishes I made, some came true for me.
The perfect rainbow touches the ground, looks like a half-moon,
that masterpiece will disappear so make your wish soon.
The color of blue in this heavenly display means loyalty.
Light blue is the color of our sky.
Green to us brings calm and serenity.
Yellow to me stands for a bright and happy day.
Red is the reflection of the sun giving life to us.
Gold portrays all the dreams and wishes we have.
A rainbow is God's gift and treat for our eyes.
So be happy, make a wish when looking up to the skies.

The history of man-made boats is awesome,
it started with hollow tree trunks for some.
At the time of Jesus there were boats for fishermen,
what stories they could tell about where and when.
The biggest boat at the time was "The Ark of Noah".
Each child and we adults learned about the story,
about Noah's instructions and not to worry.

Since ancient times boats were always improved,
the curiosity of men and designs had to be moved.

Watching the waters of lakes, rivers or oceans,
one sees all kinds of boats in motion.
I love to watch the sailboats anchored or at sea,
they have that quiet beauty and eye appeal to me.
Just to marvel and enjoy the handsome crew,
wanting to say "Ahoy Captain", and how are you?
The control and decision is in the hands of the Captain,
to navigate through calm waters and storms now and then.
The motor brings the sailboat in and out of the harbor,
the mighty wind and sails will guide until the use of anchor.

God's speed to you "Captain Nickie" of Hilton Head Island!
I pray he will take you only through safe waters,
and your sailing brings joy to you in your sailboat quarters.

That final good-bye to parents and family member,
who loved us since we were children, always we will remember.
To say good-bye to our first love or true friend,
we shall never forget that special one, but cherish to the end.
When husband or wife say good-bye to their children,
due to selfish ideas or abuse is the reason.
We adopt puppies, kittens or other pets,
they become family members, taking care of them is without regrets.
At times casual or life long friends do change,
we do not understand when they do act strange.
Holding someone's hand when death is near,
when the end comes, saying good-bye to someone dear.
If ever your heart is troubled, pray to God he will listen and hear.
During our school years we become friends with our classmates
and that special teacher's advice will be with us when going on dates.
Sometimes we meet a stranger whom we think we met before,
from the start we feel comfortable and at times more.
At the airport, bus, boat or train,
it's hard to say good-bye, who knows if we will meet again.
For some folks saying good-bye is easy!
A sincere heart will keep that special deep feeling,
the sadness of a broken heart takes time for healing.
Yes, to say good-bye could mean that all is over,
it is final and we lost that four-leaf clover.
The above happens to each of us, and do not disagree,
if you were spared so far, it still can happen, just wait and see.

BUILDING A BRIDGE

When it rains children enjoy building a bridge across a gutter,
with different ideas, what good thoughts one might utter.
Perhaps that is where Johnny became inspired to build a bridge,
he and his friends spent many hours to choose a plan, but which?
Building a bridge can have different meanings,
could be an overpass with high ceilings.
On the other hand a bridge connecting a bay,
would be wonderful and a touch of beauty we say.
To see the Golden Gate Bridge for the first time,
is an eye filling, may it always be safe from crime.
For many years there was in existence the London Bridge,
then disassembled, rebuilt in Arizona by someone rich.
Across the Hudson River is a bridge named after our first president,
there to honor George Washington who was our friend.
A bridge does not have to be constructed of cement and steel,
families and friends lose contact, a phone or letter make it real.
During a war loved ones can be separated for a while,
thanks to Red Cross and other organizations answers will come in a file.
The airplane is that bridge between foreign nations and states,
across oceans and continents to reunite at airport gates.
When thinking of someone far away and who is dear,
our memories of them and good times will bring them near.
We are blessed by God with compassion and a kind heart,
no one knows when we take that final journey and it's time to part.
So let's cherish every day on this earth,
a positive outlook and faith is important since birth.

The moment we are born, life has a direction planned for us!
There could be obstacles to overcome,
with guidance of our parents, hopefully we have a good home.
When the age is right to apply for a job,
each one of us has that dream to succeed we do hope.
Some are lucky to have an excellent education,
others try hard and can not afford a wonderful vacation.
The younger generation believe that the company of seniors is boring,
if they remembered grandma's and grandpa's look, it was so adoring.
Today's society does not recognize the multiple knowledge of the elderly,
one has to be attractive and young to be accepted or to be on TV
Some people are afraid of the thought of getting old,
it's a privilege to experience the full cycle of life, there are stories to be told.
When that first gray hair appears and we look into that mirror,
be grateful to God the years were a gift, and not filled with horror.
In our senior years our hair turns to silver and lines show in our faces,
just remember the good times, the experiences and happy places.
Retirement years are suppose to be the Golden Years,
to be healthy, content and not filled with tears.
Lucky are the people who have their mate, a pet or a good friend,
to walk beside them filled with love until the end.
All of us who have the good fortune to reach old age,
take life in stride, for many of us will not make it to that stage.
I thank God for each hour and day,
He gave me a good life so I would like to say.

THE MEANING OF VALUE!

The meaning of value can be various,
it applies to so many things which are funny or serious.
To me the importance is the value of good health,
money can not always restore good health even with acquired wealth.
That solid marriage, and the next generation of a family,
the security of a job, a house and a car makes all so completely.
Looking through the album of photos so carefully collected over years,
brings back memories, we laugh, but sometimes cry some tears!
Quiet time to think or listen to beautiful music,
we feel so relaxed and at peace, that sound is oh so classic.
Then there is that special feeling when walking through the woods,
the majestic trees, the birds, perhaps a deer, the breezes smell so good.
Oh how I love the sound of waves, and walking along the ocean,
it becomes a special treat for me to see birds and boats in motion.
To watch a live performance at the theater shared with good company,
is a true experience and will always be in our memory.
To many people money and material things seem to replace God,
if only they forgot to be so selfish, for God is good.
To have a best friend that you completely can trust,
gives one such comfort and good feeling, for each of us is a must!

And not to forget that loyal look of a pet,
so loving and gentle, return their affection and there will be no regret.
For our existence there has to be healthy water, food and good air,
so please, let's do our best for mankind, only that is fair!

Peace to all!

It was a sad day when we learned that you were gone,
for all over this world your compassion and love was known.
We shall miss your smile so vibrant and sincere,
your eyes reflecting your soul, wish you were still here.
To children and very ill people your hugs represented love,
your gentle hands holding the forgotten, yes, love you had
plenty of.
Princess Di, even though your life was a troubled one,
it gave you strength to turn things around and tried to help
everyone.
Your dedication to charities, to fight hunger and disease,
God gave you a Big Heart, and your determination would
not cease.
Being among patients of dreaded illness came to you so natural,
God Bless you, for you made the short time they had left so
special.
You were a diplomat through the world and not appointed,
your actions were real, your hunger to help others, you were
anointed.
The love for your two sons was genuine,
Prince William, please continue your mother's teachings for
all time.
Your short troubled life Diana, was filled with deceit by
people you did trust,
Thank God, for a while you found true love, so sorry it
could not last.
To many people of this world you were a God-send,
God called you so soon, for your mission here came to an end.
We shall remember you Dear Princess Di, for future
generations,
the impact and impression you left with people in every nation.

Rest In Peace!

Two friends and their dogs on their autumn morning walk,
enjoying that clean air, and here and there we talk.
It was early in the morning and after a while,
this big surprise at a distance "A Double Rainbow", wow—it made me smile.
I never saw such beauty before, Oh Lord please let there be more!
Our little valley is nestled among rolling hills,
with scattered ranches on them and a couple of windmills.
There are horses grazing, and down the road are many cows,
you see we live in the country with various animals such as meows.
Wish you could share the sight of that field of wild sunflowers,
the breeze causing to tilt their heads,
looks as though they're wishing us a good day and happy hours.
Passing by two churches of a different faith,
they look so peaceful in that early morning haze.
On our way home the bright sun lighted up our valley,
children going to school, some seemed in a hurry.
My friend and I agreed this will be a special day,
oh yes, so filled with nature all the way.
I wish to thank you Lord, from my heart to you,
for letting me admire everything that's created by you!

SIZE DOES NOT MATTER

I watched a Sparrow-Hawk waiting for the kill,
two brave Sparrows tried to attack him, they had a strong will.
You see these little birds had no fear,
this was to show that size does not matter here.
A mother does whatever to protect her children at all time,
her instinct tells her not to be afraid her love will prove all
is fine.
Athletes are called heroes and most of them are tall,
what they do well, is chasing the ball.
A small country church has that quiet and happy environment,
these mega churches have no continuity and little contentment.
A big house will be noticed from the bottom to above,
what good is it, if inside is a lack of love?
Years ago on every street corner was a "Mom and Pop store",
they knew their customers by first name, that was quite a
chore.
Today all stores lost that human touch,
everything is numbered and priced, really not fun to watch.
Diamonds come in various colors and size,
but the smaller ones have that fire and look like clear ice.
The Giant Sequoia trees get admired in awe,
how about that little fruit tree so busy and without a flaw.
People always reach for that beautiful apple or otherwise,
the look can be deceiving, for inside could be a big surprise.
In the animal kingdom the larger species get most of the
attention,
all these cuddly little critters hear "How Cute", people will
mention.
So let this be a lesson to the Sparrow-Hawk,
these little Sparrows show action and they do not talk.

THAT FAR AWAY HORIZON!

When looking at the horizon as a little girl, I did not understand,
for I thought then, as far as I could see, beyond that was the world's end.
Later in school I learned that the world is round,
and that the horizon is only part of it I found.
How exciting and perfect and mysterious happenings,
new developments in all countries and strange planes get wings.
The scientists so dedicated to mankind, and give so much of his or her life,
to find that special cure for diseases so people will survive.
Every country has gifted people, such as writing beautiful music,
listening to special pieces or songs, could make me feel homesick.
There are many famous museums all over this earth with pieces of art,
this took love, appreciation and hard work, to know where to start.
In the morning the horizon looks so blue and clear,
as though it had a good rest during the night, and there is nothing to fear.
Will that new day bring happiness to all, or sorrow?
Millions of people of this planet will not see and enjoy tomorrow.
To see that mighty sunset on the ocean or sea,
the distance looks forever, only water, it looks awesome to me.
Songs have been written about that mysterious horizon,
so perfect and all that knowledge combined and layer of ozone.

Perhaps with research in all directions,
we shall understand the happenings of the weather and
detections.
When I was young I had dreams to leave my homeland,
I am happy I undertook that courageous step,
and all the experience expanded my horizon!

The first accomplishment for little girls and boys, is to have
a friend,
the parents approve and yes, the friends can spend a weekend.
Starting at a young age we learn to give and take,
being selfish and hard to get along with would be a mistake.
But children are children, and sometimes they want too much,
there is always one special friend with whom we stay in touch.
As we grow older, we meet friends who have different ideas,
that sometimes could bring us to questionable areas.
Becoming an adult, well we are more careful of whom we
choose,
preferably honesty, trustworthy, and full of respect,
if we misjudge there will be disappointment and heartaches
when we lose.
Friendships can be fickle, many do last for years,
I am so grateful, thank you "Best Friend" for being there
through fears and tears.
You are selfless and of quality that makes a "Life Long
Friend",
Just know that I will be to you a loyal friend until the end.
Our friendship endured for almost half a century,
may God bless both of us, with many more years and free
of worry.
I wish that every person could have a friend as I have in you,
for a true friend is a gift from heaven, and the sky is blue!

LEAVES

God blessed the world with beautiful trees and vegetation,
his special touch gives to us what we need for good health and meditation.
We learned from the original creator the source of oxygen, the gift of life,
that is why we received trees and leaves, without them we could not thrive.
The Lord in his wisdom precisely chose what shape of leaf
would become any tree and plant best,
we people in the womb received various colors of eyes and hair,
well, we all know what's in between, and so goes the rest.
In spring the leaves unfold in different shapes!
The trees look alive again, and they look fully dressed.
In summer we thank the leaves for the shade, which is so fine,
the rain on the leaves pronounces the green and makes them shine.
That special magnolia tree and the leaves of the oak, even poison ivy,
leaves of a palmtree in shape of a fan looking so attractive.
Pinetrees, called the evergreen, at Christmas we enjoy again and again,
even when the countless needles fall off we shall not complain.
The dainty leaves combined with the flowers, bushes and climbers,
oh, the lovely camellia, gardenia, wisteria and honeysuckle,
give to us the unique fragrance and some do look like old timers.
The beauty of the morning sun rays piercing through the trees,
bringing colors and "That Last Hello" to us from these autumn leaves.

The cycle comes to an end when dead leaves fall to the
ground,
nature is taking back the fallen foliage to renourish the soil,
that long winter's rest will strengthen the trees
and in spring the trees and all vegetation will look sound.

We love to look at you from start until you finish your cycle,
to see that quarter moon until full moon, then you reverse
the title.
Even children point toward you, saying mommy look up
there—
with the same excitement, mom and dad reply, yes, the
mighty moon is here.
You look so spectacular when completing full moon,
songs were written about you and that harvest moon.
On a crystal clear night you appear as the owner of the sky,
millions of stars and some other planets saying to you "Hi".
Of course many clouds travel through our world's element,
at times a veil of theirs will cover your magnificent existence,
but suddenly you shine through from the ever so far distance.
By listening to a scientist I learned that you are three billion
years old,
only God can give a life time guarantee, you are a gift, you
were not sold.
President Kennedy had the faith to send men to the moon's
surface,
thank God for brilliant minds and skilled people so it could
take place.
Only you beautiful moon have the power to control the oceans,
you know the correct time to set "Tide", and "Ebb" into
motion.
Years ago through a telescope I saw part of you and some
craters,
I was so moved by that, then I knew that work was of our
creator.
Some day perhaps we people of this earth will learn,
and explore the whole territory of the moon is our concern.

I shall never forget seeing mankind and footprints in your dust,
to watch Moon Rover and the American flag, are they still
steadfast?
Now we look forward to the early evening when you start
living again,
for you will be a new moon, you are never the same.

A GLOOMY DAY

After all the wind and rain it looked like a lovely morning,
then around mid-day the sun disappeared without any
warning.
The clouds moved in, and pretty soon a gloomy day arrived,
that sky looked unfriendly, and of sun we were deprived.
I guess here in California we are blessed with good weather,
for routinely we wake up to you sun, and we enjoy that better.
Everything looks so different on a gloomy day,
the garden and its flowers do not know what to make of this
day.
Even we people at times are touched by this gloom,
sometimes we are not as cheerful, we will predict doom.
We turn to hobbies, music or watch that favorite soap,
which changes the entire day, being busy is good medicine
for us to cope.
Looking out the window, yes that splendor is absent,
we miss you sun, please let us feel that you are present.
Now that winter is here, the wood burning in the stove is
welcome,
but too many people out on the streets are not warm, only
some.
Anything living needs your warmth and sunshine
we look forward to tomorrow and all will be fine.
I pray to God, that he will take care of the poor,
for they are close to his heart, bless them and give them more.

My sister, my brother and I grew up near the river "Rhein",
To see the castle "Drachenfels" and the "Rhein" was a
favorable place of mine
The seven mountain range, each had their own name,
The stories of Brothers Grimm mentioned in detail
how Siegfried slew the dragon and all its fame.
Playing along the river and choosing that special flat stone,
when thrown across the water would jump on and on.
To watch the white steamers and cargo ships,
the river looked like a busy waterway many people took trips.

My mother's place of birth was close to the "Mosel" river,
which is also famous, but mostly for growing wine,
vineyards along the river looking so tidy, the grooming was
done at winter time.
In fall is harvest time including hard working days,
when the grapes are picked and the wine is on its way,
the celebration begins thanking God for the harvest when
they pray.
It is a must for tourists to visit the city of "Trier",
the Romans lived there, advanced beyond knowledge about
that time,
they built then, the "Porta Negra" meaning Black Gate, to
this day looks fine.
In the country one enjoys much greenery,
also ample of history and culture plus lovely scenery.
As a young adult I left the place where my roots where
established.
I am proud of my homeland, and this poem will be published.

The first adventure on my own,
was to acquire a mountain cabin with a fireplace made of stone.
Just to visit Pine Mountain Lake—
A resort with all amenities, and long walks one could take.
To have a picnic or play games along the shore of the lake,
or rent a canoe or sailboat, to miss that thrill would be a mistake.
To me the area was like God's country,
and only 25 miles from the beautiful place "Yosemite".
So tranquil and serene,
nature at its best, really a sight to be seen.
Surrounded by evergreens and old oak trees,
occasionally a deer and its fawn would visit with ease.
Enjoying the decks in front and one side,
beautiful birds sitting real close, so tame and not afraid.
My haven was comfortable and not large in size,
a cozy kitchen and two bedrooms, to me it was like winning a prize.
While walking my dogs I collected pretty rocks as souvenirs,
also gathering pine cones for the fireplace when winter was near.
When the snow fell it was so peaceful and quiet,
it looked like "A Winter Wonderland", a place to be desired.
Inga's haven was mine for seven years, they passed by so fast.
Precious memories at times I relive, but always shall last.
That seven hours drive from L.A. County was truly worth while,
for on arrival, looking at my haven filled me with pride and a big smile.

A POSITIVE ATTITUDE!

To me the meaning of the words Faith, Hope and Love,
represent such a power over all they encompass,
I believe these three words were chosen by the Lord above.
They express that there are great things and thoughts to look forward to,
if coming from the heart, these words can change lives and wishes come true.
I have taken solace in these mighty words,
it made a difference in outlook and taking care of hurts.
A positive attitude in one's life can help to lift that heavy burden,
it has to be learned, so try, there will be sunshine and faith, hope and love.
Yes, "Faith" can help us even wishing on a falling star,
will discover who it is we really are.
"Hope," will give us strength and will make us pray,
God will listen and will send answers our way.
The word "Love", oh what would anything alive do without?
We were created by love from our father and mother,
there have to be caring, kind words, commitment to each other.
For true love reflects well being,
and that special gleam in our eyes,
let's always nurture that special feeling, let us be wise!

GOSSIP!

The word gossip is such a simple word,
but how dangerous gossip can be all of us have heard.
Some people take pleasure in destroying someone's good
name,
once the harm is done, their lives will never be the same.
The expression goes "Where there is Smoke, there is Fire",
passing judgment before there is proof should not be for hire.
Gossip starts merely with thoughts that are treacherous,
God gave us a conscience so let's use it and avoid a mess.
I heard being said that the tongue can be sharper than a
sword,
this perfect organ should not be abused, it is a gift from the
Lord.
Rumors are empty talk, and let there be peace,
look for good in people, and gossip must cease.
Some humans thrive on seeing wrong in what people do,
no one is perfect, these busybodies have their own dirt to
attend to.
Thank God that each of us is an individual,
we form our own lives and do what comes natural.
The news media seems to enjoy to hurriedly report the worst,
without having facts, guessing and accusing, just wanting to
be first.
When I attended night school to learn basic English,
the teacher taught us "One is Innocent until Proven Guilty".
Gossip is going out of control, let's reverse it that is my wish.

When first we heard your name mentioned on TV,
we did not know what to expect of you, we had to wait and see.
your name is "El Niño" translated in English meaning The Son,
well, whose son are you? A mighty giant, you do not depend on the sun.
You are unpredictable, bringing heavy rain, the wind whipping the Pacific,
causing floods and mountains to move, it is and was horrific.
You traveled from a far away distance,
and our beautiful Pacific Ocean had little resistance.
Along the west coast you visited every state,
properties were damaged or destroyed,
crops were lost, that was our fate.
We were at your mercy "El Niño", you turned out to be a monster,
today the sun shines, what a lovely day; it was like a roller coaster.
Your fury "El Niño" is getting to be too much,
just calm down, we want you to leave, we like the gentle touch.
Your visit will be recorded in history books,
we shall remember you "The Evil One", that is how it looks.
May this terrible experience not visit too many places,
I pray that you lose your power, and people will have happy faces.

Some young people try to please their friends in all they partake,
it could look like fun, but also turn out to be a big mistake.
The youth of today have little knowledge in judgment,
so, feeling good and trying what is cool, are ignoring their talent.
Yes, parents try to tell their children do not do this or that,
but the answer is, do not tell me what to do, I want fun and to not be sad.
Through experience all of us will learn whom to trust,
we want to believe what is told to us, on occasion it will be unjust.
Over the years at times I was reluctant to take a chance,
whether to relocate, change of job, I sort of gave it a glance.
By taking our time to study what is best, let's practice patience,
praying to our heavenly father, and perhaps we will see his guidance.
The burden of life can at times make us feel weary,
a good night's sleep will help us to see things more clearly.
It will be a lift to our spirit and give us a good attitude
to overcome, and some things will look cute.
Mistakes do not have to be bad, can prove to be a lesson.
We learn every day, and perhaps avoid the environment or wrong person.
I have made mistakes along life's journey, but did realize,
that by some of them the reward was a big surprise!
I learned not to be too proud to admit making the wrong decision,
the wrong can be made right, and about life I have a better vision.
Going through our life's cycle is only once, let's give what it takes,
do our best and not be afraid of making mistakes.

SEA SHELLS

Just looking at various types of sea shells in my collection,
makes me wonder who was the tenant of this creation.
The species come in various colors, shape and design,
I am so proud of them the pleasure is all mine.
Wish I knew all the names of the ocean's species,
it would mean so much for I really appreciate you beauties.
From my friend I learned the story of the two sided Sand Dollar,
the story is so touching, in my possession I have two, thanks to her.
There are larger shells left behind on the beach,
placing one to our ear, hearing a sound, the ocean is not out of reach.
This shell looks like art, representing the front of this enclosure,
looks as a blossoming flower from start to total exposure.
Some black colored shells appeared while walking through the sand.
The tranquillity of the sound of water and waves in motion,
what a sight the tide left there for us,
I felt like a child, deciding which shell to take,
the ocean and its waves were so generous!
The substance of all you fantastic shells to me is a mystery,
so complete and lovely, you will exist longer than the next century.

Young boys and girls love to watch airplanes,
in their hearts they feel like pilots when playing games.
We just experienced "The Winter Olympic Games" in Japan,
how each participant had their own dream and special plan.
That baseball, football or tennis player,
start with imagination, and at times they say a prayer.
A performer filled with such big ideas,
needs discipline, and study this field covering various areas.
I love music, wish I could have learned to play the piano,
yes, I admire talented musicians, listening warms my heart so.
Sometimes such real and special people come into our life,
they seem so perfect, and leave quite an impression,
kind deeds and words, from this a rather pleasant world
could arrive.
When adopting a pet we can imagine the tricks and love they
show us,
buying certain toys, teaching that puppy may take a lot of fuss.
In thoughts listening to the waves of that river or lake,
makes me feel like being there, no matter what it will take.
Children and adults have memories of a wonderful place,
why not dream or imagine, and our thoughts even aim for
outer space.

The excitement of a mother giving birth, then holding the
baby close to her heart,
her hands touching that precious gift of love, baby and she
will never part.
How adoring the mother takes and holds her baby's hand.
Oh, they look so beautiful she declares, and mother and
father are content.
Hands are part of our human body, and so important for us
to function,
our fingers with our unique fingerprints do show a lot of
action.
From our heart and mind we receive the message to give
that loving touch,
to each of us at the right or important time will mean so much.
We need strong hands to obtain and keep our job and being
employed,
to have the means for our family, which will make us feel
overjoyed.
Holding hands across the table, and giving "Thank you" to
God,
praying alone at home we extend our hands for the good
health we got.
When saying "The Pledge of Allegiance", over our heart
we place our right hand,
to show respect and the serious meaning which will never end.
We carry small and heavy loads, children and whomever
needs our assistance,
it will give pleasure to us, and that good feeling of reassurance.
In everything we do and touch, our hands are involved,
students doing their homework or that letter needing a problem
to be solved.

I do remember my mother's strong hands and all they could do,
the hard work, she never gave up, and always was there for me and you.
Our hands should and ought to be helping hands,
not just think of ourselves, be ready for our pets and friends.
God's plan for our hands was only doing good, and never to exercise violence!

To a wife or husband that perfect partner is a treasure,
oh yes, they do exist, and they do enjoy great pleasure.
On that Birthday, Valentine's Day or Anniversary,
with a card, flowers or special gift they share their love so tenderly.
An inexpensive gift can mean so much when it comes from the heart,
after all, the thought behind it, plays the important part.
I cherish the souvenirs and various trinkets in my display cabinet,
which were given to me by my dear friends, whom I shall never forget.
In each of our lives, God sent a very special friend to walk with us,
facing problems and happy times, our "Rock of Gibraltar", without a fuss.
Sharing a treasure with someone, perhaps the gold nugget that was found,
that river or the old gold mine which today is still sound.
Even in the deserts people sift the dirt, and look for the unexpected,
they are completely engrossed in what they are doing, as if directed.
A treasure can be described as being wealthy,
but it can mean so little, when one is not healthy.
A coin collection so carefully assembled over the years,
or that crystal, the fine china when it breaks could bring tears.
The compliments and awards that were sent our way,
were such an honor so remember, they are with us to stay.
That special flower and the hummingbird in my flower bed,
I treasure, and none more beautiful I have seen yet.

ART

To watch an artist prepare for that masterpiece,
in his or her mind they envision what the eyes will please.
The easel is ready, and the canvas in place,
with skill, the artist brush in hand, soon we will see a face.
The colors look delightful, and blended so perfectly,
the brush strokes, and the picture in entirety have the look
of beauty.
Now the matching frame will give the finished appearance,
that happy look in the artist's face, reflects full acceptance.
For me the ultimate treat was to see and admire,
"The Mona Lisa" on display, was my desire.
Only "Leonardo Da Vinci" knew the secret of that charming
smile!
Each museum has a wealth of works of famous artists,
to visit, spend time, to look and study, and understand I insist.
Someday I hope to see in person "The Sistine Chapel" so,
in renaissance style, to marvel the creation by "Michelangelo".
Art comes in so many different forms and shapes,
one could spend a fortune, looking and collecting for that
special taste.
To really understand art, takes a lengthy education,
for each artist has that original idea and own explanation.

It feels like yesterday but two years ago, I had this great vacation,
with old friends whom I had not seen for years across the nation.
Sitting in that airplane on my way home and looking at the beautiful sky,
the clouds were snow white, and looked as if they wanted to play.
So my thoughts went to prayer, I felt that you listened to every word,
this last poem in this book, I dedicated to you "My Lord".
I told you about my wonderful vacation, and what I would like to do,
putting all these recent memories in thoughts of poetry, but there is you.
I explained my lack of experience, and asked for help in words and title,
thanking you God somewhere over the states, waiting for my first title.
The next morning the words "Precious Gift of Friendship" came to me,
it was like saying notice me, yes, I asked for this and replied oh I see.
So I gathered my thoughts, and with your guidance from above,
I started to write poetry, and discovered this is what I love.
All 50 poems came and were written straight from my heart,
I share with the readers, what being with old friends can start.
We reminisced and laughed, by now our hair is gray,
some were teenagers when first we met, we all came a long way.
They came through ice and snow, and made me feel welcome,
sharing about these years that passed by, I felt so at home.

It saddened me to say "Good-Bye", for who knows where
and when,
we will meet again, we live on opposite coasts, we will try if
we can.
Thank you God for the faith I have in you,
you are "Alpha and Omega" and you inspired me to write
as I do.